I

THE CHAMPION RULES

Karen Putz

(In loving memory of my nephew, Kevin Griffard)

Copyright © 2022 by Barefoot Publications

All rights reserved. No part of this publication may be reproduced, distributed, or transmitted in any form or by any means, including photocopying, recording, or other electronic or mechanical methods, without the prior written permission of the publisher, except in the case of brief quotations embodied in critical reviews and certain other noncommercial uses permitted by copyright law. For permission requests, email to the publisher, addressed "Attention: Permissions Coordinator," at karen@agelesspassions.com

ISBN: 979-8366096386 (Paperback)

ISBN: 979-8366102315 (Hardcover)

Any references to historical events, real people, or real places are used fictitiously. Names, characters, and places are products of the author's imagination.

Front cover image by Karen Putz

Book design by Karen Putz

Printed by Kindle Direct Publishing, in the United States of America.

First printing edition 2022.

Barefoot Publications

New York

THE CHAMPION RULES
(of Life)

Be on Time

Be Coachable

Be Passionate

Be Helpful

Be Committed

Be Persistent

Be Resilient

Be Approachable

Be Grateful

Be a Humble Champion

This book is dedicated to all of the barefoot water skiers who have taught me the Champion Rules.

FOREWORD BY KEITH ST. ONGE,

2X WORLD BAREFOOT CHAMPION AND 24X GOLD MEDALIST

I'm Keith St. Onge and since the age of ten, I had a dream: I wanted to become a National and World Champion Barefoot Water Skier. Through a lot of hard work, determination, practice, and stumbles along the way—I became a World Champion, twice. I also hold 24 World Championship gold medals.

Karen and I met at my ski school in Winter Haven, Florida, where she showed up for a barefoot water ski lesson. At the age of 44, Karen had a desire to return to the sport that she had long ago abandoned as a teen. On her first try, she put her feet in the water and stood up. Her passion for the sport returned right then and there!

For two and half years, Karen interviewed me while writing my memoir, *Gliding Soles*. In our work together, I shared many of my own "Champion Rules" while teaching and training Karen to compete in barefoot water ski tournaments.

Karen knows all about following dreams and what it takes to become a Champion. She may not be a World Champion in a specific sport, but she chose to follow all her own passions in becoming a Champion in life. The student has now become a teacher of the Champion Rules.

All of the "Champion Rules" which this book outlines can give you a direct path to success in anything you choose to do in life. Some of these rules may not be a natural part of your life at first, but with determination, commitment, and resilience—anything is attainable.

A NOTE FROM KAREN PUTZ

At the age of 44, I took up barefoot water skiing again.

I say "again," because it had been many, many years since I put my bare feet on the water.

But, let's go back to the beginning. I was born with normal hearing and started losing my hearing in elementary school. I grew up being quite ashamed of being hard of hearing, despite having a deaf and hard of hearing family. I tried my best to hide my hearing aid. I often bluffed my way through conversations, trying very hard to fit in with people who could hear.

My older brother, Kenny, was a barefoot water skier. I enjoyed watching him on the water and I wanted to learn. I tried over and over to learn how to kick off a ski without success. One summer, I begged my mom to buy me a kneeboard. After a couple of tries with the kneeboard–I finally stood up on my bare feet. I loved the sport! It was also fun being the only girl on my lake able to barefoot water ski.

Then one day, I decided to cross the wake–a trick I had done once before–only this time, I told my driver to go much faster so that the wake would be lower. I pulled myself far away from the wake and aimed toward it way too fast. My left foot caught the wake. I took a hard fall and cartwheeled a few times. When I climbed into the boat–I was deaf.

As you can imagine, my life became quite dark at that point as I struggled to adjust to a new reality. One morning, I woke up and decided to embrace the journey of being deaf. I signed up (pun intended!) for a sign language class and learned to communicate in a whole new way. My life took an amazing turn at that point as I met some wonderful deaf and hard of hearing people–including Joe–the guy who became my husband. We have three kids who are now young adults. Ironically, I passed on a very rare mitochondrial gene to my children–and all three are now deaf. The gene is so rare that we are one of just four families in the world identified as carriers and we happen to be the only family in the United States with this particular gene.

I had abandoned the sport for many years until I tried to barefoot water ski the day before my 44th birthday. I could not even stand up on the water. A few months later, Joe sent me a link to a TODAY Show which featured a 66-year-old woman barefoot water skiing. Judy Myers started the sport at the age of 53!

I reached out to connect with Judy via Facebook. Judy invited me to come down to Florida and learn how to barefoot water ski again. I flew down during my kids' spring break. Judy introduced me to Keith St. Onge, the 2X World Barefoot Champion. Keith gave me a quick lesson on the dock and we headed out on the lake. The moment I put my feet on the water and stood up, my passion for the sport came flooding back.

Keith, Judy, and I became great friends. Both of them became wonderful mentors and taught me a lot about life–both on the water and off. We trained together and competed for several years. Many of the lessons shared in this book are from both of them. The lessons are also from *many* of the barefoot water skiers I met throughout the years, both at competitions and from barefooting in different states. Some of the lessons are from other mentors, as well.

All of the lessons in *The Champion Rules* are lessons that apply to life. No matter what path you choose in life, if you apply the lessons from this book—you, too, will become a Champion of life.

CHAPTER 1
Curiosity Leads the Way

Samuel Watkins pushed off the curb with excitement. This was the first time his parents had allowed him to ride his bike around the neighborhood alone. His family recently moved from South Carolina to Winter Haven, a small town in Florida.

"Remember, stay on this street and go on the same path that we've ridden together before," his mom reminded him. "I'll be right here, waiting for you."

As Samuel pedaled, sweat began to drip down his back. The sun belted out 92 degrees with no wind—typical weather for a Florida morning. As he rounded the first corner, he heard the roar of a boat engine. Samuel stopped to watch. A water skier zipped by, doing 360-degree turns on top of the water. A few short seconds later, the skier threw the handle and sank into the water. The boat circled back toward the skier in a slow arc.

Samuel was intrigued. The skier did not seem to have anything on his feet. He wore a cobalt blue sleeveless wetsuit with yellow, orange, and red stripes running down one side. As the boat circled around the skier, he grabbed the handle that was floating on the end of the line.

The boat engine roared again. The skier laid back in the water with his feet crossed over the rope. As the boat pulled him forward, the skier sat up and rode on top of the water as the boat gained speed. Suddenly, the skier put his feet in the water and stood up. Samuel's mouth fell open. The man was water skiing on his own feet!

Samuel watched the skier put his foot in the handle and turn around on top of the water. He continued to do various tricks and turns for a few seconds. Once again, he sat down on the water and tossed away the handle.

"Samuel!"

He turned at the sound of his mother's voice.

"What are you doing? I was looking everywhere for you! I was getting worried because you were gone so long."

"I'm sorry, Mom. I was watching this water skier. Look! He's water skiing on his bare feet."

Once again, the boat engine roared. Samuel and his mom watched as the water skier danced on the water, turning to and fro.

"That's very interesting—I've never seen anything like that before."

"I want to try it," Samuel said.

"Let's try water skiing with skis on your feet first," she laughed.

"Can I? Mom? Please? I really want to learn how to water ski on my own feet."

"I'll see if I can find a place where you can take lessons. Meanwhile, let's get back to the house and unpack a few more boxes. We can start painting your room this afternoon."

Samuel was an only child. His parents tried for years to have children, and his mom miscarried twice. Samuel had an older brother, Liam, who died shortly after birth. "Liam is your Guardian Angel," his mom often told him. "Anytime you feel scared or unsure, you can talk to him and he will give you the answers you need."

Samuel talked to Liam all hours of the day, but especially at night after his mom turned off the lights. There was something comforting about having a brother to talk to, even if he wasn't physically there.

Samuel's dad took a new job as a Project Manager for a local manufacturing company. They had always loved Florida—they stayed at an Airbnb in Key West every year.

Samuel's mom popped open the can of paint and stirred it with a wooden stick. The color was "Nantucket Blue," and it reminded him of water. Samuel couldn't stop thinking about the man who was water skiing on his bare feet.

Who was he? What was his story? How did he learn that unusual sport?

"Mom? Can we take another bike ride later? I want to find that water skiing guy."

His mom laughed. "You're still thinking about water skiing? Let's get the first coat on the walls and then we can take a ride. But don't forget, you need to do today's lessons."

Samuel groaned. Today was math and science day—two subjects he loathed. Fortunately, being schooled at home meant that he could finish his assignments quickly. Samuel loved to draw and paint. He was always finding ways to incorporate art into his studies, especially when it came to math.

It was late afternoon when Samuel finished his studies. "Can we go for a bike ride now? Or can I go by myself again?" Samuel pleaded.

"I'll join you," his mom chuckled. "I've never seen you so excited about a sport before."

There was no one on the lake when they rounded the curve. Samuel was disappointed. As they rode down the winding road, his mom spotted a sign.

"Look, Samuel!"

A wooden sign stood in the middle of a yard. "Winter Haven Barefoot Water Ski School."

Samuel's heart started to beat faster. *This was it!*

"Mom, can we stop in? Please?"

"I suppose we could."

They walked their bikes up the long driveway. A tanned, young woman in a tank top was sweeping the sidewalk leading up to the deck. "Well, hello there! I'm Nikki." She held out her hand. "What can I do for you?"

Samuel didn't say anything. His mom broke the silence. "Hi, I'm Mary. This is my son, Samuel. He was watching a water skier on the lake this morning and wanted to learn more about the sport."

"Oh, that was Kevin Langston you saw this morning. I was driving the boat. I noticed you watching from the road," Nikki smiled. "Kevin is the seven-time World Champion barefoot water skier. He's the best skier in the world. He owns this school. Do you want to meet him?

Samuel nodded. "I want to learn how to water ski on my feet."

"Have you ever water skied before?"

"No, but I really want to do it on my bare feet like Kevin did this morning."

"Honey, I think you need to learn how on skis first," his mom said.

Nikki laughed. "Actually, we like it when they've never skied before—there are no bad habits to unlearn. So, let's get you signed up for a lesson. I think we have an opening tomorrow morning. Let's go inside and I'll check the schedule."

They stepped into an office with a large teak desk in the middle of the room. A set of bare feet was carved into the legs of the desk. Every wall held ribbons of medals hanging down from the top of each wall. One wall held a teak shelf filled with trophies from one end of the room to the other end. There were 4 x 4 photos of barefoot water skiers covering all four walls.

A slim, yet muscular man walked in. "Hi there, looks like we have a new visitor! I'm Kevin. Welcome to the ski school. So, who do we have here today?"

"I'm Samuel. I was watching you this morning. It was really cool to see you water ski on your feet."

"Samuel is ready for a lesson," Nikki said. She flipped through a calendar hanging on the wall. "And you're in luck—we have one spot open in the boat tomorrow morning at eight."

"I'll be there!" Samuel said. "If that's okay, Mom?" He gave his mom a pleading look.

His mom smiled and nodded. She tried not to show her concern at the high price of the lesson. "I don't really know anything about this sport. Is it safe? It seems like you were going awfully fast out there."

"It's a fast sport, but we take safety seriously," Kevin said. "We've had skiers as young as four. Our oldest skier is actually 91 years old—and he still competes in tournaments."

"Kevin started barefooting at ten and I started when I was eight," Nikki said. "You could say we really love this sport!"

"What Nikki hasn't told you yet, she's the Women's World Barefoot Champion. No other woman in the world can beat her. In fact, she can out-ski 98% of the men!"

Nikki laughed. "I like beating the guys! You're all set, buddy," Nikki clamped her hand on Samuel's shoulder. "We'll see you here tomorrow morning at eight, sharp. First rule of a champion—**Be on time.**"

Samuel was so excited. He couldn't wait to get on the water. He went to bed early and tossed and turned all night. He could not seem to shut off the excitement bubbling up within him. At the first crack of dawn, he was up and ready to go. He didn't need the alarm to wake him up. He grabbed a banana and his bag.

"Don't forget to take a towel," his mom reminded him. "And the zinc sunscreen. You're going to be out there for three hours. I don't want you getting burned. I'll ride over with you, and you can ride back home afterwards."

CHAPTER 2

A Passion is Born

Kevin and Nikki were waiting on the deck when Samuel walked up. Two other guys were putting on wetsuits.

"Right on time, Samuel!" Kevin smiled. "Very good! As you know, the first rule of a champion is always be on time. Now, I want you to meet Jim and Brent. Jim is from Connecticut and Brent is from Canada. They are training for an upcoming barefoot tournament. They're both 18."

"Welcome to the sport," Jim said as he shook Samuel's hand. "We always have fun on the water. Watch out for Brent, he tends to hog the water time when it's warm out. Sometimes we have to pull him off the water. It's always cold up there in Canada, you know."

Samuel laughed.

Nikki handed Samuel a wetsuit. "Here, try this on and see how it fits. It's going to be a bit tight at first, but once you get in the water, it'll loosen up."

Samuel wiggled into the wetsuit and Nikki helped him

zip it up. It was so tight that he had a hard time breathing at first. He followed the men down to the dock.

"Now, before we jump in the boat, we are going to talk about the second rule of a champion," Kevin said. "The second rule…'**Be coachable**.' What this means is that you'll need to keep an open mind and listen to what I'll be teaching you. If I can't coach you, then we're both wasting our time on the water—and we surely don't want that, do we?"

For the next ten minutes, Kevin showed Samuel the different positions he would have to go through to be able to stand up on the water. Over and over he practiced until Kevin was satisfied.

"Okay, buddy, you're ready to get on the water. Hop into the boat."

Jim and Brent were already sitting in the boat and they greeted him with big smiles. "I remember the first time I tried barefooting," Jim said. "It took me a few days to finally learn how to stand up on the water. I bet you'll be footin' before the end of the morning."

As Kevin maneuvered the boat away from the dock, Samual suddenly had a thought. "Kevin, are there alligators in the lake?"

Kevin laughed. "Yes, there are alligators here. They won't bother you, though. The boat engine scares them away. We've never had a problem with them and in the history of water skiing, no one has ever been attacked."

Samuel disliked alligators. The reptiles actually terrified him. And today, he was going to get in the water with them. Kevin's words were somewhat reassuring. Samuel was just going to have to trust him. Plus, the excitement of the new sport outweighed the apprehension churning within.

Kevin brought the boat to a stop at the other end of the lake. "You're up first, Jim. Same practice as yesterday."

Jim flung the rope out of the boat and jumped in the water. Kevin slowly idled the boat forward. Samuel watched in fascination as Jim hooked a foot on the rope and turned over upside down.

"What is he doing?" Samuel asked.

"He's about to barefoot water ski backwards," Kevin said. He pushed the throttle forward. Jim took both feet off the rope and put his toes down in the water as the boat accelerated. For a few seconds, there was nothing but spray—and then Jim rose up out of the water, skiing backwards on his feet. Samuel watched as Jim lifted one foot and then crossed both wakes.

"This is called 'slalom.'" Kevin shouted. The roar of the engine made it difficult to hear.

Jim went back and forth across the wake in rapid succession, lifting one foot out of the water then putting it down and switching to the other foot before crossing again. A few seconds later, he let go of the handle and slid into the lake.

"How long does it take to learn slalom?" Samuel asked. "I want to learn how to do that!"

"One step at a time, buddy," Kevin chuckled. "Everyone goes at their own pace. The back slalom is one of the many advanced skills in competition."

Kevin turned the boat around slowly and cruised back toward Jim.

"That run was much better, Jim! I want you to put your foot down earlier on the next run and start your cut quicker. That will give you another point."

Then it was Brent's turn. Brent worked on his turns, doing 720 degree turns in one direction then the other. Samuel glanced at the speedometer. Forty-five miles per hour!

"Does this hurt your feet?" he asked as Kevin slowed to a stop.

"Only if you do it long enough!" he laughed. "A competitive run is only 15 seconds long. You have to do as many tricks as you can or cross the wake as many times as you can– in just 15 seconds. We have another kind of competition called 'Endurance' tournaments. You ski until you fall or let go. Now, those can hurt—you can get some big blisters on your feet!"

Brent did a few more runs and climbed back into the boat with a tired smile.

Kevin pointed to Samuel. "Ok, buddy, you're up! Now, remember the steps we went over this morning. Go slow. And be patient!"

Samuel slid into the water and grabbed the boom—a straight, metal bar that was attached to a pole in the middle of the boat. He put both feet on a cable wire which connected the boom to the boat.

"Remember, lean back until the boat starts to go—then the three-point position--and put your feet gently but firmly on the water."

Samuel tightened his grip and nodded.

A few seconds later, Samuel stood up on the water. *He was barefoot water skiing on his own feet!* He grinned from ear to ear. The guys in the boat yelled and cheered.

A minute later, Kevin motioned to Samuel to let go.

Samuel let out a whoop as he sank into the water. He could hear the guys hollering and cheering once again.

"This is awesome! I want to do this again and again!" Samuel said as the boat came near. He did two more runs, each one was longer than the other.

"On this next run, I want you to put your feet closer together and shift ninety percent of your weight to your right foot and just ride it as long as you can," Kevin said.

Samuel followed his instructions and in a moment of impulse, he lifted his left leg. Kevin gave him a thumbs up sign. He was water skiing on one foot! The cheers from the boat were so loud that they drowned out the roar of the engine.

At the end of the run, Samuel didn't want to let go, but he could feel his foot starting to burn. It felt like a dozen razors scraping against his foot.

"That was absolutely fantastic!" said Kevin. "Come on in the boat and take a rest."

"Hey Sammie Boy, you have a natural talent for this sport!" Brent said. "I don't think I've ever seen a student do all of that in one set without falling!"

"I want to learn more!" Samuel said. "That was the most fun I've ever had."

During his second set, Samuel fell twice. The first fall caught him completely by surprise. Samuel slammed into the water and tumbled head over heels. When he finally came to a stop, he was coughing and sputtering.

By the time the guys finished three hours later, Samuel was exhausted but elated. The sport demanded intense concentration every second on the water. As they idled back to the dock, Samuel peeled off his wetsuit.

"You did great today, buddy!" Kevin said. "How are you feeling?"

"I loved every minute of it. It was so much fun. When can I do it again?"

"Well, we will have to talk to your mom about that. You can take regular lessons with us each week if you'd like. You'll need your own wetsuit. I can see you have lots of enthusiasm. That leads us to the third Champion Rule: **Be Passionate**. I can see you have passion inside of you.

Passion is fuel and it will push you along. Be safe riding home. Have your mom give me a call this afternoon and we'll see what kind of lessons we can set up."

Samuel felt like he was flying as he pedaled home. He burst into the house with such high energy that he startled his mom in the kitchen.

"Well, how was it?"

"Mom, it was awesome. I stood up on my first try. I even barefooted on one foot! It was so much fun. Can I take another lesson tomorrow? Kevin said for you to call him this afternoon to set up regular lessons. Mom, please? Can I?"

His mom smiled. She had never seen Samuel so excited about a sport.

"I'll give Kevin a call and see what we can work out. It's certainly not a cheap sport, but I'm sure we can set something up."

"You can use my allowance. I can mow lawns to earn extra money."

"Sit still long enough to eat lunch and do your English this afternoon, and I'll give him a call."

CHAPTER 3
Building a Foundation

Time slowed to a crawl as Samuel sat on his porch to read and finish his English homework. One of his assignments was to write a 500-word biography about a famous person. He typed in "Kevin Langston." For the next hour, he immersed himself in learning everything he could about the champion water skier.

Kevin grew up in Ste. Genevieve, Missouri, a sleepy little town just west of the Mississippi. His parents owned a small cottage on a private lake. The lake was owned by a friend of Kevin's father. There were just seven houses on the lake and all of the neighbors were good friends. Many of them worked at the Mississippi Lime company in town. They all lived for the evenings and weekends on the lake. Three of the men and two of the women loved to barefoot water ski.

One July evening, Kevin's father asked him if he wanted to try barefooting. The lake was calm and the sun was low in the sky. Just like Samuel, Kevin picked up barefooting on his first try. By the following summer, he entered his first competition. He went home with a third place medal—only because there were just three skiers in his age division.

By the time Kevin was sixteen, he won his first Overall medal and became the Junior World Champion. The following year he joined the Pro division and took the gold in the National tournament. No other skier could beat Kevin. Year after year, he took the Overall medal in the Nationals and set record after record. He won the World Championship a total of seven times, losing twice to his rival, Zaine Phillips.

Zaine was an excellent skier and the competition between them was fierce. Often just a few points separated the two men. Zaine was much younger and Kevin figured it was only a matter of time before the scales would begin to shift. At forty-two, he was the oldest competing athlete in the pro division. He was the only skier in the world who held a record in all three divisions of slalom, tricks, and jump.

It took Samuel just a short time to finish his essay and he discovered he had over 3,000 words typed out. He had never been so intrigued in doing research for a school project as he had with this one.

His mom came into the room just as the printer spewed out the last of his assignment.

"My goodness, what did you write about?"

Samuel smiled.

"You wrote about barefooting, didn't you? Well, I have

some good news. I just got off the phone with Kevin and we set up some lessons. You can go three mornings a week. There's another kid—another 13-year-old from the neighborhood who will be joining you."

"Aw, thank you, Mom!" Samuel jumped up and hugged her. He handed her his assignment. "Can I go for a bike ride?"

She nodded. "Just stay in the neighborhood. Don't go out by the main street."

Samuel hopped on his bike and went straight to the ski school. The school was empty, but Samuel heard the boat engine in the distance. He walked down to the dock and watched as the boat zipped by. This time, Nikki was in a wetsuit with a helmet perched on her head. Samuel watched as Nikki crouched low and approached a small ramp. Suddenly she popped into the air with her legs behind her, almost as if she shot out of a cannon. A few seconds later, Nikki landed on her feet and skied away. Over and over, she blasted off the ramp. Twice, she crashed into the water head over heels as she landed.

A few minutes later, Kevin was behind the boat and he sprang off the ramp just as Nikki did. He flew higher and longer—landing gracefully in the water with hardly a splash. There were two other students and they crashed over and over as they went over the ramp.

"Samuel!"

Samuel turned at the sound of his mom's voice.

"I've been looking everywhere for you!"

"I'm sorry, Mom! I just stopped to watch Nikki and Kevin. It was so cool—they were jumping off a ramp with their bare feet and flying through the air!"

"Samuel, you've been gone for over an hour. I was worried! You can't just go wherever you want as long as you want. We are still new here in this town. Now, get your bike and let's head back. You'll be back here soon enough on Friday."

On Friday morning, Samuel was up before his alarm clock rang. It was still dark outside and he could hear the patter of rain on the roof. *Would he be able to ski today?*

He walked into the kitchen just as his mom finished a call.

"I just called Kevin as I wasn't sure if they were going to ski in the rain, but he said as long as there is no lightning, they are skiing," his mom said. "I'll drive you over and pick you up afterwards."

Samuel wolfed down the scrambled eggs and toast and grabbed his bag. As his mom drove, he thought about the Champion Rules.

Be on Time

Be Coachable.

Be Passionate.

"Good morning, Samuel!" Kevin was standing at the end of the dock next to a tall, lean kid with a shock of white hair. "I want you to meet Jordan. He lives in the next town over. He's been footin' for a while—how long has it been?"

"Three and half years now." Jordan said. He gave Samuel a quick handshake. "Hi, Samuel, nice to meet you. How long have you been skiing?"

"I just started two days ago."

"Oh, a newbie! Well, we should have some fun in the rain this morning."

"It's supposed to clear up soon, but yes, you're right—let's go have some fun, boys!" Kevin said. "But before we begin the fun, we have some work to do. The boat runs on gas, not air. So, I want each of you to grab a gas can from the shed and meet me at the boat."

The gas can was heavy, and with each step, Samuel's arm ached as he shuffled toward the dock. Jordan was way ahead of him—he moved as if the can was as light as a feather. Kevin was waiting in the boat, holding a large umbrella. Samuel watched as Jordon emptied the can quickly into the side of the boat.

"Okay, Samuel, it's your turn. Follow Jordan's lead and then we'll be on our way.

Samuel struggled at first, but when the gas began to flow through the plastic pump, he let out a relieved sigh.

"Great job in being coachable!" Kevin said. "Let's get the cans back in the shed and then we'll head out.

Samuel watched in fascination as Jordan went through his trick routine on the water. Even though he was thirteen years old, he had competed for three years. Jordan was considered the next rising star among barefoot competitors. Like Samuel, Jordan was schooled at home, along with three of his siblings.

"Okay, Samuel, today we are adding a short rope with a handle. This is a different way to start from what you learned two days ago, but the basics are the same."

Samuel struggled to stand up in the water. Getting up on the water using a rope was much more challenging than holding on to the boom. He bounced up and down as he tried to maintain his balance. Over and over, Samuel's feet slammed into the water and he tumbled head over heels to a stop.

After several tries, Samuel was out of breath. He was frustrated at his lack of progress.

Kevin tossed him a pair of shoe skis. Samuel looked at him with disappointment. "That's not really barefooting if I have to wear those things," he said.

Kevin laughed.

"Patience, Grasshopper! When it comes to barefoot water skiing, you'll have to build a solid foundation with one skill set before you can move on to another. Without a foundation, you'll make all kinds of mistakes. A house built on a poor foundation will crumble. We don't want that happening to you."

Samuel started to open his mouth to protest, but then he remembered the Champion Rule:

Be coachable.

He put the shoe skis on and practiced getting up over and over, using the five-foot rope. Every now and then, the shoe ski caught a tip on the water and Samuel fell flat on his face. By the end of the morning, Samuel was getting up on the water without training shoes and barefooting short distances. It was an amazing feeling to glide on top of the water on the soles of his feet.

"Job well done, buddy!" Kevin clamped a hand on Samuel's shoulder. "You've been very coachable today!"

Samuel smiled. He was glad he kept his mouth shut and listened to the World Champion.

The next morning, Samuel groaned as he got out of bed. Every muscle in his body was sore. He had never felt such aching pain in so many body parts at once.

"Are you okay, son?" his mom asked.

"Yeah, just a little sore." He didn't want his mom to know the truth.

"Here, use some Arnica—that will help you bounce back quicker." Samuel's mom was a Reiki master. She loved using oils and natural products for health care.

"Now, I know you probably want to head over to the ski school to watch the guys again, but today, we start a new science module. We will be joining a group of homeschoolers at the Community Center."

As soon as they walked in, Samuel spotted a familiar face. "Hey Mom, that's Jordan over there!"

"Why don't you go say hi while I sign in."

Jordan looked up with a big smile as Samuel approached. "Hey, footin' buddy! I was kind of hoping you'd be joining us homeschoolers here."

Hanging out with Jordan made the time go by quickly. The two boys discovered they both had a love for space and astronomy.

"Did you know there's been several soft landings on Mars–but no human attempt yet," Jordan said. "I want to be among the first!"

"I'd be a little scared to be the first," Samuel said. "I'll go–after you come back safely!"

Jordan laughed. "I like your humor!"

The conversation soon turned to barefoot water skiing.

"Do you get nervous when you compete?" Samuel asked.

"Oh yeah, every time! Kevin once gave me some great advice. Right before my first tournament, he told me that it was okay to have butterflies. You see, butterflies are a sign that you're about to perform something big. And there's a secret--you harness their power by imagining all of them flying in formation!"

Samuel laughed. The idea of having butterflies line up in perfect formation was something he never imagined before.

"When is your next tournament? I would like to go and watch you--and to see what it's like."

"We have a local tournament coming up this Saturday at Paradise Lake. It's about an hour from here. You can ride with us. Kevin, Nikki, and Rocky will be competing, too. We usually go out to dinner afterwards—it's a lot of fun. Hey--we even have a Boom Division for beginners—you can compete, too!"

"I don't know about that, I just learned to barefoot!"

"Oh, we have newbies all the time! Just think of the fun you'll have. All you have to do is stick your feet in the water and stand up. You already know how to do that!"

"Ok, I'm game!"

And just like that, Samuel signed up for his first tournament.

CHAPTER 4

Everyone Starts as a Beginner

At Friday's training, Kevin taught Samuel a few new tricks to prepare him for the tournament. Samuel learned how to sit down on top of the water and stand back up again. He learned how to let go with one hand and wave. He also learned how to do a small hop on top of the water.

When they arrived at Paradise Lake early Saturday morning, the water was as smooth as glass. Two boats were docked near the shore. A small crowd of skiers gathered at the registration desk. The stands were filling up with fans and supporters.

"After you've signed in—go put your wetsuit on and head down to the dock," Nikki instructed. "The Boom division is first. Just follow the trick order that we taught you yesterday. And Samuel…go out there and have fun!"

Samuel's hands were shaking a bit as he pulled on the wetsuit. He wasn't sure if it was from excitement or nervousness. He was the third skier in line when he arrived at the dock. The other skiers were ten years old. He watched as they took off and did their tricks. They looked confident and comfortable on the water.

Samuel closed his eyes and tried to imagine all the butterflies in his stomach flying in formation. None of the butterflies would cooperate–his stomach felt like a jumbled mess.

"Go, Samuel!"

Samuel turned at the sound of his dad's voice and glimpsed his parents in the stands. They waved enthusiastically.

"I see you brought your cheering section," Nikki grinned. "Let's get out there and stand up on the water. You're up!"

Samuel slid into the water and grabbed the rope attached to the boom. He unhooked the handle from the boom and crossed his legs over the rope.

"I heard this is your first tournament," the driver said. "You got this, buddy! Are you ready? What kind of start and what speed do you want?"

"A medium to 36," he said. Just as Kevin taught him.

He gripped the handle tighter and took a deep breath.

"In gear," Samuel said.

The boat took off as soon as Samuel gave his signal. It took all of Samuel's concentration to focus on the task ahead. His legs felt like rubber as he placed his feet in the water and stood up. For one brief second, he celebrated. In a flash, he tumbled face down into the water.

Samuel coughed and sputtered when he surfaced.

"Caught a toe, didn't you!" the driver laughed as he idled back toward Samuel. "Don't worry. It's your first tournament and it's all about learning. Just relax and stand up your second run. And remember, your job is to go out there and have fun."

The second run was a repeat of the first. This time, Samuel was mortified at falling twice. He was sure everyone was laughing at him, but in the distance, he could hear cheering from the stands.

"That's a good start, Samuel! You stood up both runs," Kevin high-fived him as he walked up the shore.

"I can't believe I fell both times," Samuel said. "That's a little embarrassing."

"Hey buddy, you just started out! You're learning. You'll bounce right back and do better on the next one! Now, let's get out of your wetsuit because I've got another job for you--you're going to be a 'Score Runner' today." Kevin handed over a clear tube with a screw-on top. "Every time the boat comes in, you hand over the new tube and take the other tube from the boat crew. You'll run the tube over to the Scorer's tent so they can tally up the scores. You see, that's another Champion Rule—**Be Helpful**." When you help others, you truly become part of a team and you make an impact.

"I'm happy to help," Samuel said. He peeled off the wetsuit and pulled on his t-shirt. He stood at the back of the dock, waiting for the next skier to come in. Samuel enjoyed the task of running the scores up to the Scorer's tent.

When the Open Pro Division began, Samuel was fascinated at the high level of skill each skier demonstrated on the water. Samuel watched as Rocky, Kevin, and Nikki took turns competing. Nikki captured first place in the Women's division. Jordan captured first place in the Junior division. He was the rising star that everyone was watching. His goal was to replace Kevin as the World Barefoot Champion someday.

In the Open Pro Division, the race for first place came down to Kevin and Zaine, an experienced skier from Texas. Zaine was ten years younger than Kevin. He was known for his cocky attitude and bold freestyle moves on the water.

"Zaine has the lead. I think Kevin is going to take second." Samuel overheard two skiers talking.

"It might be time for the old man to retire," the second skier said. "Kevin can't keep up with the younger crowd anymore. He's getting slower on his turns."

As he headed back down to the dock, Samuel watched Zaine and Kevin as they stood and waited for a skier to come in. Zaine was a bundle of nervous energy, jumping up and down on the dock. Kevin had his eyes closed, trying to drown out the incessant chatter around him.

Both skiers were down to their final event.

Zaine did both of his runs flawlessly. He danced around as he came out of the water.

Kevin knew he had to ski harder than he had ever skied before to claim the coveted first place. He executed his first run perfectly. On the second run, Kevin fell on one of his turns. A hush fell over the crowd. On the dock, Zaine let out a whoop and pumped his fist in the air. The first place medal was his.

Samuel watched as Kevin smiled and waved as he rode back to the dock. If Kevin was disappointed, he certainly wasn't showing it.

At the awards dinner that evening, the mood was light-hearted and the room filled with laughter. It was easy to see the flow of camaraderie among the barefoot water skiers. Samuel received a t-shirt with the inscription: "I survived my first barefoot water ski tournament."

On the way home, Samuel reflected on the events of the day. Even though he fell on both of his runs, he felt like today was one of the greatest days of his life. He wanted more. He wanted to learn how to fly through the air off the jump and do turns on the water.

Samuel wanted to be a World Champion.

"Good morning!" Kevin greeted Samuel with a smile. "Now that you have your first tournament behind you, the real work begins. We're going to make sure you never fall on a start again."

It was a grueling morning. Kevin dragged Samuel up and down the lake on his feet at various speeds. Excruciatingly slow and then blazing fast. Kevin made Samuel execute his trick run over and over. By the end of the training, Samuel's arms and legs ached. He grabbed a quick lunch and he was back in the boat for the afternoon session.

"We're going to do the same thing again, this time on the short rope."

"My legs feel like rubber, I don't think I can even stand up on the water," Samuel said.

"If you want to be a champion, buddy, you've got to push yourself through this. The only way you'll know the limit of what you can do is when you go beyond what you think is possible. Suck it up, Buttercup. We've got some work to do."

Samuel stifled a groan and zipped up his wetsuit.

To Samuel's surprise, halfway through the afternoon, he found a "second wind." Each run became easier and Samuel stood up with confidence. Over and over, he was able to do his trick runs without falling.

"Okay Sammie Boy, we're going to change things up. I

want you to use the long line and I'm going to teach you how to barefoot water ski behind the boat."

Samuel was excited. As he floated in the water waiting for the boat to pull ahead, he closed his eyes and visualized every step that Kevin taught him. The rope tightened. He was ready.

"Okay!"

The boat pulled him out of the water with a roar. Samuel sat up and rode over the wake. Just as he had visualized, Samuel placed his feet in the water and stood up.

He got up on his first try! He was barefoot water skiing behind the boat! He could hear the boat crew cheering over the noise of the engine. Samuel held on to the handle as tight as he could. He didn't want this moment to end.

Everyone cheered when Samuel climbed into the boat. "I guess you're not so tired anymore," Kevin grinned.

"I feel like I can do 20 more!'

When they arrived back on shore, Kevin motioned Samuel to sit down on a bench. The other skiers had left.

"What did you learn today, buddy?"

"I learned that I could do much more than I thought I could."

"What would have happened if you gave up after the first session and went home because you were tired?"

"I would have missed out on a great moment," Samuel said. "I would have never skied behind the boat."

"And you would not have known what you were capable of doing. You see, you created new limits today by pushing past what you thought your limits were. This brings us to another Champion Rule: **Be Committed**. It is the commitment that sees you through. When you give up, you lose. When you commit, you succeed. You're learning the Champion Rules pretty fast! Now you can go home and be sore all you want. Good job, buddy!"

Samuel continued to push the limits, learning new tricks each day. Every morning, he was filled with excited energy and he couldn't wait to get on the water. One month later, he was barefoot water skiing backwards on his feet behind the boat, learning how to slalom back and forth.

At the very next tournament, Samuel took fifth place. He didn't get a medal, but he knew it was only a matter of time before he took his own place on the podium.

CHAPTER 5

The First Step to an Authentic Life

One afternoon after training on the water, Kevin motioned to Samuel to follow him in the office.

"Hey Samuel, have a seat. I have a question for you. Have you heard of a Life List?"

Samuel shook his head.

"First, tell me, what is your big goal for the next tournament?"

"I don't want to fall on my runs!"

"What would the opposite of that be?"

"Well…I would finish both runs with the handle in my hand."

"That feels a lot more positive than falling, doesn't it? You see, Samuel, everything is energy. The boat you ski behind is energy. The water is energy. You are energy. Here's the thing, what you focus on, expands. When you focus on a negative outcome, everything becomes about avoiding that negative result. When you focus on a positive outcome, you can only expand it better and better. How many points will you get if you do your runs the same way we've been practicing?"

"I would have 1000 points."

"That's right! So now you have a measurable goal to work towards. Now that you know which tricks will add up to 1000 points, you can focus on those tricks. You will know whether or not you meet your goal by the number of points you score at the next tournament. To be a champion, you must have goals to work toward and they must be written in such a way so that you know you've achieved them. Now, today, I'm going to show you how to create a Life List."

Kevin handed Samuel a bright blue, leather-bound journal. The first ten pages had lines numbered up to 100.

"This is your Life List journal. In the next couple of days, I want you to write out what you want to BE, DO, and HAVE in your life. Write them out as sentences--as if you are already living those things. Here's why we do it that way; when you write as if you are already living your dreams, the universe responds to that language."

"Can you give me an example?"

"Sure. When I first started my Life List, I was writing things like, 'I will be the class president.' It is far more powerful to write 'I am the class president.' When you write as if it is true in your life, it becomes true."

"I see."

"Now, you don't have to show me any of this. It's for you. It's your life map. The thoughts, goals, dreams, wishes that you have inside of you are there for a reason. Your job is to get those dreams out of your head and into your journal. Just remember, there is power in the written word and when you write things down, you have a guide for your life."

Kevin pulled out a journal from the top desk drawer. The leather cover was slightly faded and the pages were worn and rumpled. " My Life List has over 100 items, but I'm going to start you with 50. My father gave me this when I was in high school. Take a look at the very first entry."

Samuel looked at the list.

I am a World Champion.

"I wanted that more than anything else in my life," Kevin explained. "By writing down all the BE, DO, HAVEs --I identified what was really important to me. Knowing yourself is the first step to creating an authentic life. Many people skip this important step and they drift through life. They're like a boat drifting down the lake, going with the wind. They don't clarify what they want from life and *how* they want to live it. As a result, people just live the same day over and over and then they get to the end of their life with a lot of regrets."

"How many of the 100 things have you completed?" Samuel asked.

"I've experienced 87 from my current list," Kevin smiled. "I know this, because I use the Life List as a guide. I am on my third list now. The list grows and changes. I keep it in front of me so that my life is aligned with what I have on the list. Instead of wasting time on things that are not meaningful to me, I delegate those tasks to other people or I do them efficiently. You see, every decision you make is either getting you closer to the life you want--or further away. And here's another thing...God delivers the timing. I trust that what's on my Life List will unfold in divine timing."

Samuel left the ski school and pounded the pedals toward his house. He could not wait to start on his Life List. Once he arrived home, he grabbed a pen and headed out to the back porch and sank into a wicker chair. The hot Florida heat dripped sweat off his forehead as he wrote out his dreams. Samuel was surprised at the different thoughts that came to him as he wrote. Some of the ideas were things that he had never considered before--such as riding in a hot air balloon, taking a pontoon ride to his favorite restaurant on the lake, and becoming a seaplane pilot.

At the end of the second hour, Samuel looked at his list. He had written 32 items. He grabbed his mom's phone and called Kevin.

"What's up, buddy?" Kevin answered on the first ring.

"I wanted you to know that I did the Life List, but I only came up with 32 things. I just couldn't come up with any more things to add to the list. Why is that?"

Kevin laughed.

"You're just starting out on your journey. As time goes on, you'll evolve and change--and so will your Life List. This is an ongoing process--you'll keep adding to it as you learn more about yourself and the world. For now, everything you've written is designed to serve you where you are in life. Focus on that. Meanwhile, I'll see you in the boat tomorrow morning. Be ready, buddy-- we're going to work on surface turns."

Samuel couldn't believe it.

One of the items on his Life List: "I do surface turns with ease."

The next morning, Samuel could hardly contain his excitement when he stepped into the boat. For weeks, he had watched Jordan do one turn after another on the water. Jordan was no longer skiing in the Junior division. He qualified for the Open Men's division and was quickly rising up in the ranks. He was traveling to tournaments out of state and bringing home one medal after another. The next local tournament was just a month away and it was the final tournament of the year. Samuel was looking forward to his next tournament. The long practices on the water gave him more confidence and he was itching to rack up better scores.

But today, he was going to learn yet another new skill.

"Go put your shoes on," Kevin instructed. "Once you learn how to turn on the shoes, the same principles apply on your feet. It's like riding a bicycle--you're on the training wheels for a short time and then you learn to ride."

Dreaming of turns and actually trying to do them were two different things. The first time Samuel tried to turn, he smacked into the water so hard that he saw stars. The second time was worse--he caught the edge of the shoe on the water. When he surfaced, Samuel was having second thoughts about learning turns. He felt shaky and disoriented.

On the next run, Samuel could not let go of the handle to begin the turn. He was scared to fall. Up and down the lake, Samuel tried to rack up the confidence to release the handle and turn on the water.

The longer he waited, the more the fear escalated. Up and down the lake, Samuel bent his knees and tried to find the courage to turn. He could see Kevin's impatience as he continued to hesitate.

Samuel finally closed his eyes and tried to turn.

Smack!

The brunt force of the water felt like hitting concrete. Samuel's neck ached. He wasn't so sure that he wanted to learn this new skill after all.

Kevin motioned him into the boat.

"Let's talk about what you're feeling," Kevin said, as they idled back to the dock. "What's going through your mind?"

"I'm not feeling confident," Samuel said.

"What are you feeling?

"I'm…I'm scared to let go of the handle."

"What you're experiencing is fear," Kevin explained. "What do you fear most?"

"Falling."

"But you've already done that, right?" Jordan said.

"Well, it hurts to fall!"

"No one ever said this was going to be easy," Kevin laughed. "Fear is simply a thought in our heads. Fear comes from the unknown--not knowing what will happen *and* not feeling in control of what will happen. Fear is what holds us back from moving forward with what we really want. In your case, what do you *really* want?"

"I want to learn how to turn without falling."

"Remember how we talked about directing your focus? What's a more positive way of reframing that thought?"

"Well, I want to be able to turn with confidence and ease."

"That's a lot more positive than focusing on not falling, right?"

Samuel smiled.

"Now, you see, confidence and ease can only come from practicing and refining the skills you need," Kevin explained. "This means that the only way around fear is smack dab right through it. You've got to set up the foundation for the turn and then let go of that handle with confidence. This means that even when you feel the fear, you'll need to reach deep down inside to pull out the confidence and override the fear. Jordan, how long did it take you to learn this?"

"I'm still learning it!" Jordan laughed. "I think it took me a year and half to do turns with some confidence. Even now, the confidence comes and goes."

"So, Samuel, you remember that Champion Rule: **Be Committed?** Let's go deeper with it. We can look at this in different ways. Commitment comes from knowing what you want and sticking through the ups and downs to achieve the outcome. Commitment is also the promise to yourself to do what it takes to accomplish a result. What would happen if you hesitated in the middle of a turn?"

"I would fall," Samuel said.

"Exactly. Commitment sees you through from the beginning to the end result. Now, without commitment, there is no strength."

"What do you mean?"

The lack of commitment is a weakness. I want you to imagine that you have one foot on the dock and the other foot in the boat. What would happen if the boat started drifting away and you kept one foot on the dock and one foot in the boat?"

"I'd probably fall in the lake," Samuel laughed.

"That's right! When you commit, you put your energy all in one direction instead of splitting up your energy. That's what makes you stronger."

"I still struggle with commitment," Jordan laughed. "It's probably one of the hardest things to do. Sometimes, on a tough day, I just want to give up. Kevin always reminds me to keep my focus on the plan--and my goals."

"All right, we are done with turns for now," Kevin said. "Commit to next time."

CHAPTER 6

The Competition is You

Samuel stood on the dock zipping up his wetsuit. The butterflies in his stomach fluttered. He closed his eyes and pictured them flying in formation, giving him the energy he needed to get through the tournament.

He felt different.

The many weeks of practice gave him a foundation of solid skills and a new confidence. He was turning on the water with ease and completing his tricks faster and faster.

"Visualize every second of your run," Kevin reminded him earlier. Samuel pictured himself completing every trick in his run and finishing with the handle in his hands.

"Remember this: you are not competing against your opponent," Kevin said. "You are competing against yourself. Your goal is to be better than your last run. Always strive to push your *own* boundaries and set new records for *you*."

Samuel was ready. He was going to go out there and ski just like he did in practice–with confidence.

"In gear," he instructed the driver.

As the boat pulled forward and the rope tightened, Samuel took a deep breath. He gave the go ahead to the driver. This was it.

Fifteen seconds flew by. The second run felt even faster. With a triumphant grin, Samuel tossed away the handle and slid into the water. He completed every single trick in both runs! His slalom runs were even better--Samuel crossed the wakes faster than ever before.

"Hey buddy, you're catching up to me, quick!" Jordan said when Samuel arrived at the dock. "It won't be long and we'll be competing in the Open Pro division together!"

Kevin and Nikki rushed up with big smiles. "Sammie Boy, that was incredible!" Nikki said. "All of your hard work really paid off. You looked super confident throughout all of your runs and you had that handle in your hands the entire time! We are really proud of you!"

"How do you feel?" Kevin asked.

"I feel great!" Samuel grinned. "A heck of a lot better than I did at my first tournament, that's for sure!"

"Nice job! All of your hard work is paying off. Come and follow me, I want you to meet some skiers."

Samuel followed Kevin to the stands. An older woman

with short white hair and a man with gray hair were sitting on the bleachers chatting.

"Hey Judy and Jim, I want you to meet Samuel. Sammie Boy, meet the world's oldest competitive barefoot water skiers. Judy started barefooting when she was 53 years old. She's now 72. We call her "The Old Lady," but she's anything but old! Jim started when he was 40 years old. He's now 90 and still competing. He needs a little help getting into his wetsuit, but watch out when he's on the water! He has not missed a single National tournament since his first competition."

"Wow, that's truly impressive," Samuel said. He shook their hands. "It's an honor to meet both of you. I am impressed at the number of years you've been on the water!"

"Welcome to barefooting! I'm sure Kevin told you the Champion Rules," Judy laughed. "That's one of the first things I learned from him! One of my favorite rules is to "**Be Persistent**," and Jim and I take that rule seriously. We keep persisting! That's how we ended up being the oldest competitors!"

"When you love the sport as much as we do, it's easy to be persistent," Jim said. "Of course, it is the energy of passion which fuels us!"

"And you know what passion really is?" Judy leaned in closer.

Samuel shook his head.

"Passion is your joy. It's a gift within you. All you have to do is unwrap that gift! That's where persistence comes in--most people give up when the work becomes too hard or when challenges come up. Think of passion as the fuel that pushes you forward."

Samuel sat and talked to the two older champions for a half hour. He was fascinated by their stories. Jim served in the Navy and he held the record for the most sit-ups in one minute. Judy had her pilot's license and flew a Piper Cub.

"I crashed my plane once," she told him. "Right after I got it fixed, I was back in the air. You can't let setbacks keep you from moving forward again.

"I want to learn to fly," Samuel said. "That is something that I have on my Life List. My father was a pilot and he used to have a small plane."

"I can connect you with Gerald--he's a seaplane pilot who works over at Lake Christie. And Gerald is also a barefoot water skier. He once pulled Kevin barefooting behind a seaplane! Ask him to show you the video sometime. They were on the news!"

Samuel watched in fascination as Judy and Jim competed. Both of them captured first place in their divisions as there were no other skiers at their ages. At 90, Jim had a hard time walking down to the dock, but he stood up on the water and barefoot water skied on the boom with a huge smile on his face.

Samuel skied his personal best and beamed when he received the Junior division third place medal around his neck. He watched as Jordan took the Overall medal. Kevin came in second place. The student had beaten the teacher. Zaine ended up in third place.

Someday, I'm going to be standing on the podium in first place as a pro.

CHAPTER 7
The Messy Middle

Life settled into a rhythm as Samuel honed his skills at the Winter Haven Barefoot School. New students joined each week as they flew in from all over the world. Samuel was fascinated with the different accents and cultures that each student brought into the boat. He learned new words and phrases in French, German, and Afrikaans.

Samuel's skills on the water continued to grow. He continued to master his turns on the water both forward and backward with confidence. The falls didn't seem to hurt as much anymore.

"Samuel Boy, put your big boy wetsuit on today--we're going to learn to jump," Kevin said."We are going to use the boom and just slide over the ramp to get a feel for it."

Samuel's eyes widened. He had been bugging Kevin to let him go over the jump for several weeks now. He had visualized himself hitting the jump and then landing on his feet every night before going to bed. He imagined himself soaring through the air just like Superman--and landing every jump.

And now the time was finally here. He was going to go over the jump! Samuel couldn't wait for the moment to put his dreams in action.

With Kevin's instructions swirling through his head, Samuel approached the ramp with confidence. His feet slid over the jump and he landed smoothly. The whole experience was effortless. Samual repeated one jump after another until Kevin was satisfied with his progress. He fell just once.

Samuel climbed into the boat with a huge smile on his face.

"Great job, my man! In all the years of training and teaching students, I've never had a student who could land jumps over and over on the first day," Kevin said. "It's absolutely amazing watching how quickly you are progressing through the jumps. You have a natural instinct when it comes to this skill."

"I feel like I was born to do this," Samuel said. "Since the first day I saw you and Nikki going over the ramp, I've wanted to do this."

"Ok, let's set a new goal," Kevin said. "You'll need to land 100 jumps and then I'll teach you the next part--how to fly through the air."

It took Samuel three weeks to land 100 jumps.

"I'm ready to fly," he told Kevin.

Turn Your Setbacks into Bounce Backs

"Today's the day you're going to advance as a skier," Kevin told Samuel. "I've been impressed with your progress on the water and now you're ready to learn how to become Superman."

Samuel's confidence on the water was at an all time high. He was able to slide over the jump during tournaments and was consistently placing well at tournaments. Even though Jordan was racking up one medal after another in the Open Pro division, Samuel's skills were catching up. The two boys were close friends, but fierce competitors. Samuel continually took second place in all of their personal challenges on the water during practice. Jordan showed no mercy in practice-- he continued to set the bar high for himself. He was chasing both Zaine and Kevin in the competitions and putting pressure on both competitors.

The boys celebrated their birthdays just two months apart.

Jordan's skills on the jump were not the best--it was a skill that he continued to struggle with. He had more crashes to his name than successful landings. It was his skill in slalom and tricks that consistently brought him first place medals.

Samuel knew that he had to master the Superman pose to be able to land a jump on his feet. Every afternoon, he practiced on his trampoline in the backyard by jumping up and pretending he was Superman before landing on his feet. Every night before he fell asleep, he imagined himself flying off the ramp. To become a champion, he knew he had to acquire this skill.

"Jumping in the Superman pose is a skill that separates the men from the boys," Kevin explained. "There is no margin for error. Every split second determines whether or not you'll land--or crash. Hop in the water, it's now your turn to fly."

The water rippled outward when Samuel jumped in. As he approached the ramp, Samuel took a deep breath and gripped the handle tightly. He rose off the ramp and allowed his feet to fall behind him. He tentatively leaned forward and then brought his feet down.

Crash.

Hitting the water at such a high speed from the air knocked the wind out of Samuel. It took him a few minutes to catch his breath.

"What do you think went wrong?" Kevin asked as the boat idled back.

"I don't think I brought my feet down fast enough."

"That's right, Everything is a split second with jumping. Let's go again."

The water felt like concrete as Samuel crashed a second time. And a third. When he tumbled to a stop after his third attempt, Samuel had second thoughts about even trying the jump again. All of the jumps he did previously did not prepare him for the feeling of hitting the water from such a high spot in the air. The confidence he felt earlier was completely gone.

"I think I hurt my ribs. I can hardly breathe."

Every breath felt like a thousand needles pushing into his side.

"Let's do it again," Kevin said.

Samuel wasn't sure he wanted to try it again. He wanted to stick with the jumping that he was comfortable with. A familiar feeling crept up.

Fear.

Samuel hesitated.

"Grab the rope, you're going again," Kevin said.

"I-I don't think I can do it," Samuel said. "It's a lot harder than I thought it would be. I need a minute to catch my breath."

"Here we go, Sammy Boy. Round Two. We're doing it again. Get the handle."

Samuel realized there was no way out. He would have to jump again. His legs felt like rubber as he stood up on the water. As the ramp came closer, Samuel clenched his teeth. As soon as he hit the air, he panicked and let go of the handle. This time, the crash was even harder.

"I don't want to do this anymore--I don't think I'm ready for this jumping," he said as Kevin idled the boat back.

"One more time," Kevin said. "Remember the fundamentals. You've landed countless times on your feet with regular jumps. We're just adding a new element to it and building a new foundation. Anytime you build something new, there's a big learning curve."

Samuel was ready to cry, but he didn't want Kevin to see any tears. He closed his eyes and took a long, deep breath. There was no way out of this. He was going to have to grit his way through it.

Once more, Samuel landed with a crash. This time, Kevin motioned him to get into the boat. With a dejected sigh, Samuel climbed in and sat down.

"Hard stuff, isn't it?"

Samuel nodded.

"The journey to becoming a champion is never easy," Kevin explained. "You're going through exactly what I went through during my journey to becoming a world champion. I almost gave up on my dreams at that point because the goal seemed too hard. The pain was too much. I bet you're hurting in more ways than one--I get it. Life is like that. We all face moments in which our destiny is shaped by the adversities we face--and how we choose to respond."

"How did you keep going?

"Well, that leads us to yet another Champion Rule: **Be resilient**. You see, that's your ability to bounce back even when things are tough. LIfe is never a smooth, easy path to reach your goals. There are setbacks, obstacles, and barriers that come up from time to time. Most people give up when the path becomes too hard. They never see the pinnacle of success. The way I look at it-- the stuff that stands in your way is a measurement of just how bad you want to achieve your goals. Becoming a champion is a big goal, and it's up to you to determine how to bounce back when you've been knocked down. So let me ask you this, do you want to become a champion?"

"Yes!" Samuel said.

"Do you want to give up and walk away from the goal?"

"No--but…"

"There's no 'but' about it," Kevin held up his hand. "Keep your focus on the goal. You're going to turn your setbacks into bouncebacks, so that one day, you'll look back and see how far you've come. Remember, this process is a journey--and the only way to get to your goal is to continually strive to be better each day. Strive to be one percent better--it all adds up. You've put in some good effort today and we are just at the beginning. Take a rest. Jordan, you're up. Now, Samuel, I want you to use this time to study Jordan's jumps--and learn from them."

For the entire spring, Samuel worked on becoming better at his jumps. The more Samuel faced the ramp, the smoother he became at soaring through the air and attempting to land on his feet. The crashes seemed to hurt less and less each time.The fear was still there--every single time--yet, Samuel managed to work through his emotions at every practice.

Then one afternoon, Samuel flew through the air and landed on his feet. It was a sweet feeling to finally ski away from the ramp with the handle in his hand. He climbed into the boat with a huge smile on his face. All of the pain from the previous crashes was now a memory. Samuel was ready to face his next goal: he was determined to land an inverted jump at the Nationals tournament that summer.

THE POWER OF HAVING A VISION

"Hey boys, stop in my office on Friday morning. We are going to take a break from the water since it's supposed to storm that day. I've got something else we're going to work on," Kevin said.

"Don't tell me you want us to sweep the Pro Shop floor again," Jordan joked.

"Or clean out the ski garage," Samuel said.

"Watch it, guys, or I'll have you cleaning out the Pro Shop toilets," Kevin laughed. "No, this time, we're going to work on something that can change your life. See you Friday morning."

Jordan and Samuel arrived at Kevin's office on Friday morning soaked to the skin. The gray skies unleashed a torrent of rain mixed with wind. Spanish moss flew off the trees and tumbled down the streets.

Kevin had a stack of magazines piled high on his desk.

"Oh, it's 'Dream Board Friday,' I see," Jordan laughed.

"Yeah, it's time for you to update yours and it's time for Samuel to create one," Kevin said. "Samuel, do you know what a Dream Board is?"

Samuel shook his head.

"A Dream Board is a visual representation of what your hopes and dreams are. You see, the visions in your mind become the realities of your life. Every dream starts with a vision in the mind. You can't have goals without a vision. You can't plan action without a vision. So today, we're going to explore some visual components of what you are hoping and dreaming about."

"I enjoy doing this," Jordan said. "When I did my first Dream Board with Kevin and a couple of things on my board came true–I started expanding the dreams on my board. It is fun to see what shows up in life when it begins in your mind."

"The power behind a Dream Board is that the visions remain in front of you on a daily basis," Kevin continued. "I keep my board in my bedroom, where I see it first thing every morning and the last thing every night. This helps me keep my focus on what I really want to bring into my life. Whenever a new distraction comes into my life, I review my board to see if it lines up with my dreams. If it doesn't, I say no to it!"

The boys spent the morning cutting out pictures from magazines and printing pictures from the web. Two hours later, Samuel headed out the door with his Dream Board tucked into a cardboard tube. He couldn't wait to get home and hang it up in his room. In the center of his Dream Board, Samuel pasted a picture of himself standing on the podium with the World Champion trophy in his hand.

On Saturday morning, Samuel's dad dropped him off at the Kendon Seaplane Training School. Gerald greeted him with a big smile as they shook hands. "Samuel, I've heard some great things about you from Kevin. Glad to have you here. This is the day you learn to leave the water for the air!" he said. "Before we begin, let's head inside. We are going to go over some of the basics."

For an hour and a half, Samuel learned the ins and outs of flying seaplanes and how to read the water.

"Before we go out, I want to show you one more thing," Gerald said. He pressed play and a seaplane flew across the screen. Kevin glided across the water on his bare feet with the seaplane towing him.

"Oh, Judy told me about this! I'm going to add this to my Life List. I want to barefoot water skier behind a seaplane!"

The two of them walked outside toward a bright yellow 1959 seaplane bobbing softly on the water. Samuel was intrigued as Gerald explained the history of the seaplane. Most of the seaplanes were originally 1940's Piper Cub planes mounted on straight floats. Unlike the modern day planes, the seaplanes were minimalistic and could be flown without the cockpit doors in place.

"Hop in, Samuel, let's hit the water--and the air!"

As the seaplane gathered speed, Samuel's heart began to beat faster. The last time he had been in a small plane, he was just five years old. His father owned a four-seater Cessna. Samuel remembered the Saturday morning flights with his parents in which they would fly for an hour or two and touch down to grab breakfast at various airports before flying back home. Two years later, his father developed seizures and had to give up his pilot's license.

Once they were in the air, Gerald showed Samuel the different lakes and explained how to find a safe place to land. "Most people think glassy water is best for landings, but those landings are actually harder," Gerald explained. "A nice, flat ripple is better."

Samuel engaged the rudder after they landed and Gerald coasted the plane back to shore. He taught Samuel how to tie down the plane. Samuel's father walked up just as the two of them finished.

"Did you have a good flight?'

"Yeah, Dad! It's like being in your plane all over again! I can't wait for the day I can fly solo!"

When Samuel got home that night, he noticed one of the pictures he had cut out and placed on his Dream Board.

It was a picture of a seaplane.

CHAPTER 8
Release the Outcome

Samuel was looking forward to competing at the Nationals in August. He was consistently moving his scores higher and higher in local competitions and taking home first and second place trophies. He had to land at least one inverted jump at the Nationals to break into the Open Pro division and pave the way to compete in the World Championships.

The smog was heavy as the plane dipped a wing toward the LAX airport. Samuel had never been to California and he was looking forward to the tournament. This would be the first tournament without his parents, but his teammates were now like family to him.

"Boys, make sure you get your wetsuit bags," Nikki reminded them. "The tournament site is two hours away and we can't come back if you forget them."

The site featured two lakes side by side. Spectators could watch events from the middle of the two lakes. The tree-lined lakes were long and narrow, making it ideal for tournaments. Samuel and Jordan headed down to the starting dock to do some practice runs.

"Hey boys, watch that backwash on your second runs--you don't wanna trip over your pretty toes."

The boys turned at the sound of Zaine's voice. Zaine was a fierce competitor with decent skills--but he was best known for trying his hardest to mess up the mindsets of other competitors. More than one skier had fallen in tournaments--simply from the power of Zaine's trash talks, which were often disguised as "helpful hints."

Fortunately, the boys knew better than to listen to Zaine, especially right before a tournament. Kevin had prepared them both well.

"Remember, the only person you are competing against is yourself," Kevin reminded them earlier. "You are striving to beat your own times, on your own runs. Stay focused on that."

Samuel did well in his practice runs, but he did not land a single jump in practice. He could not shake off the nervousness he felt inside. He tossed and turned all night, sleeping fitfully.

A light wind blew gentle ripples across the lake as the morning sun inched higher in the sky. The stands were already full and people were sitting on blankets on the grassy hill between the lakes. The first skier cut across the water, slaloming back and forth.

Samuel closed his eyes and tried to review his runs in

his mind. He knew if he could see and feel every trick and every movement in his mind, he could transfer that skill to the water. As he waited for his turn, the anxiety inside of him started to bubble to the surface.

There was a lot riding on this tournament and the pressure felt enormous. The idea of becoming a World Champion seemed so incredibly far away. Samuel had a lot of work ahead of him to even begin down the path of the World Championship. He had to do what seemed impossible for him: he had to land at least one inverted jump in the tournament and complete a set of tricks that were incredibly challenging for him.

"How's it going, buddy?"

Samuel turned to find Jim, the oldest competitor, putting on his wetsuit. Samuel could see that Jim was struggling to get the wetsuit over his shoulders."

"Would you like some help with that?"

"Sure. My hands aren't what they used to be and sometimes I think the wetsuits shrink with every tournament!"

Samuel laughed. He helped Jim zip up the wetsuit.

"Jim, after all of these years of competing, do you have a piece of advice for me? I can't seem to shake off the nerves."

"Son, when you've been competing as long as I have, there isn't much that will trigger the nervousness anymore. I will tell you this: go out and have fun. Let your passion for the sport carry you–but also release the outcome. You're not responsible for the outcome, you're only responsible for doing your best in each run. You have absolutely no control over how you place in each tournament. If you know you've done your very best and you've put your all-out effort in each and every run, then you've placed where you're supposed to place."

"That's good advice. Thank you."

Samuel watched in awe as Jim stood up on the water. Because he was the oldest competitor in his age group, Jim was guaranteed to be a champion every single time.

The butterflies subsided as Samuel zipped up his wetsuit. He was going to let go and trust that his endless hours of training would pay off. Both of his runs went smoothly and his slalom scores were a personal best. All that was left was for him to land an inverted jump.

He needed to ski away just one jump to begin his trek to the World Championships.

His first and second jumps ended in spectacular crashes. Everything was riding on his final jump. As the boat idled back toward Samuel, he started to shake.

Release the outcome.

Just ski your best and you'll place where you're supposed to place.

Jim's words echoed in Samuel's head. As the boat pulled him to his feet, he lined himself up with the ramp. Samuel flew into the air and hung for what seemed like an eternity before he brought his feet back down on the water. He held on tight as he regained his balance and skied away.

He did it! He landed his first "Superman" jump in competition!

The cheering from the crowd grew louder as Samuel slid on the water and walked up the shore.

"We have a new Junior jump record!" the announcer boomed.

Jordan ran up and scooped Samuel in a big hug and swung him around. "A record, buddy!! You set a new record and now you're qualified into the Open Pro division!"

Back home in the boat, Samuel and Jordan trained even harder than before. The two of them were now on the path of chasing for the title of World Champion. Samuel's skills on the water were progressing fast. Kevin was still taking first place in many tournaments, but the two boys were rising fast up the ranks.

During a lull in one of their practice sessions, Kevin shut off the engine.

Ok, Jordan, what's the 7th rule of being a Champion?

"**Be approachable**."

"What does that mean?" Samuel asked.

"Who is the hardest competitor to approach?" Kevin asked.

Oh that's easy, that would be Zaine."

"And why is that?"

"Well, he's always trying to mess everyone up."

"Let's go deeper with that," Kevin said. "What kind of 'vibe' do you get when you're around him?"

"I'm always uncomfortable around him and I try to avoid him. Plus he's the one who is always arguing with the judges and making trouble."

"So the vibe you're feeling is not a positive one, and thus you don't want to approach him to ask for advice or input, right?"

"Yeah." Samuel nodded.

"The seventh rule, **Be approachable**, is all about the energy or the vibe you have while around other people. When you have an approachable vibe, people are attracted to you. By being approachable, you'll connect with people who also have the same interests and passions as you. This leads to even more opportunities in life. When you are not approachable, you send off a vibe that attracts more negativity- and it becomes a cycle. People do not want to be around people who have a vibe that is unapproachable."

"So, how can I work on being more approachable?" Samuel asked.

"There are a couple of ways you can do that," Kevin explained. "First, having an open mind goes a long way. Seek to understand people by listening deeply. Practice empathy–that is the art of *understanding what people are feeling or experiencing.* When people feel heard or understood by others, that creates a connection right there. Jordan–what's another way you can be approachable?"

"Another way is by being interested in the other person–asking questions to get to know them better. When I first came here, I was incredibly shy. Kevin made me ask every new person TEN questions during every set!"

"You're not so shy anymore, are ya?" Kevin laughed. "Now, Samuel, what's another way you can be approachable?"

"How about by smiling at people? That's something my mom is always reminding me to do whenever I meet new people."

"Yes, that's right! A smile goes a long way–it conveys the message that you're open to connecting with someone."

"Especially when you have a goofy grin on your face!" Jordan stuck out his tongue, crossed his eyes, and laughed.

On a Thursday morning, the phone rang. "Samuel! It's

Gerald on the phone," his mom said. "He has something he wants to share with you."

"Hey Samuel! Can you bring your friend Jordan to the Kendon school this Saturday? Oh, and bring your wetsuits, we will do some barefooting after your lesson!"

Samuel hung up and immediately called Jordan. "Hey, I have a question for you–do you have the goal of barefooting behind a seaplane on your Life List?"

"Matter of fact, I do. Why? What's happening?"

"Well, I'm not entirely sure, but I think we just might get the chance to do that this Saturday. Gerald wants both of us at the seaplane school. You wanna go?"

"Heck yea! I've had that seaplane goal on my Life List for awhile now! Wouldn't it be cool if that came true for both of us?"

Samuel and Jordan showed up at the Kendon Seaplane school bright and early. The sun was just about to break through the clouds. In the distance, an egret swooped down and grabbed a fish for breakfast.

"Hey boys, today's a special day," Gerald said. "Today, we're going to make your dreams come true–you'll both get to barefoot water ski behind my plane! Channel 7 is on their way over, so let's get those feet ready. And just so you know, both of your parents have already signed the release. We've been planning it for weeks."

"A Life List moment!" Jordan chuckled. "This is awesome!"

"Yeah, I had a little talk with Kevin and he mentioned that both of you had a similar goal of skiing behind a seaplane just like he did years ago. So today, we are going to make that happen and have some fun while we're out there! Except, we are going to put a little twist on it–we're going for a Guinness World Record of three of you barefooting behind the plane. Bet you can guess who the third one is?"

"Heyyyyyy boys!" Jordan and Samuel turned at the sound of Kevin's voice. "Today we are going to make some history with the three of us barefooting!"

"This is crazy, but I'm excited!' Samuel said.

"Boys, this is the power of a vision board and Life List in action. You see, once you identify a dream, the universe comes together to make it happen. People show up in your life–like Gerald here–and they open doors for you. So, let's go have some fun!"

It was a magical day for the boys as they skied with Kevin behind the seaplane and checked off an item on their Life Lists.

CHAPTER 9
Follow Your Gut Instinct

Jordan and Samuel competed fiercely throughout the year. They each racked up medal after medal as they prepared for the World Championships. Jordan was the heavy favorite to win the Overall trophy. He was currently ranked number three and Samuel was ranked number ten. This World Championship tournament would be Kevin's last–he planned to officially retire from the sport after his final run. Samuel was just happy to qualify to ski in the Worlds. His goal was to score a personal best in every run.

The flight to Australia was long but very smooth. Samuel's parents joined him. They planned to stay an extra week to tour the country and see the sights. The tournament was on the Molonglo River in Canberra, a site that did not always provide optimal ski conditions due to the unpredictability of the river's flow. The trees that lined one side of the river provided a windbreak–depending on the direction of the wind.

"Don't get a mouthful of river water in you," Nikki warned. "It won't be tasty, I can tell ya that."

The next morning, the conditions were not optimal. The river was moving at a fast rate. One skier after another fell on their practice runs. In the afternoon, the wind picked up, creating white cap conditions. There was no way to continue to practice and the safety coordinator called all the skiers off the water by late afternoon.

"Come on, mates, we are going to visit some of the natives around here. Everyone piled into a rented bus.

"Where are we going?" Jordan asked.

"You'll see," Nikki said. "We are going to have a little bit of fun to take our minds off our skiing."

Nearly an hour later, the bus pulled up to the Sanctuary Nature Reserve.

"What the heck?"

Samuel turned just in time to see Zaine's face crunched with displeasure. "I don't really want to waste my time with some animals. This is total crap."

"Give it a chance," Nikki said. "You just might end up liking it."

"I came here to ski, not to be a tourist."

"Well, you can stay with the bus driver then," Nikki said. "The rest of us are going to hang with some furry creatures."

One by one, the teams filed off the bus and walked into the lobby of the Nature Reserve. They gathered around a short woman with long blonde hair holding a koala. "Hi everyone!" I'm Shayla, I'll be your Ranger Guide for today's interactive experience. Come and meet Toby. He's our oldest koala here at 21 years old. The average lifespan of a koala is about 12 to 15 years old."

"Wow! Why do you think he has lived so long?" Jordan asked.

"He's our happiest koala. He takes care of everyone else and has the kindest heart. Plus, he absolutely loves to eat. Do you want to hold him?"

Jordan held out his hands and Shayna brought Toby over. Toby sniffed Jordan's chin and then laid his head on his shoulders. One by one, a few team members took turns holding Toby and feeding him eucalyptus leaves. The energy in the room took a delightful turn–the stress of the upcoming tournament melted away. The various team members began to mix and mingle as they toured the reserve.

"Why is this area all burned?" Samuel asked, The group stopped in front of an area that was charred.

"We set controlled fires in various areas to revive growth," Shayna explained. "Most people think of fire as destructive, but it serves a purpose. That which is burned down, clears a space for new growth to begin. This practice is over 60,000 years old."

"Kind of like when Kevin makes us burn up our runs and start all over again," Samuel chuckled.

"That's right," Kevin said. "Sometimes you have to destroy what you've built up so that you can start over stronger than before."

The teams bonded and laughed as they walked through the sanctuary. When they headed back to the bus, Zaine was fast asleep in the back.

"He sure missed a good time," Jordan said.

The next morning, the river was smooth. One by one, the skiers zipped and turned on the water, competing fiercely for the coveted titles in their division. The scores were tight and to everyone's surprise, Samuel was scoring very high.

During a lunch break, Kevin came over to sit by Samuel. "How are you feeling, buddy?"

"I feel pretty good! This is definitely the best I've ever skied!"

"You are totally on fire and skiing the best you have ever done. You have come a very long way in your skiing career in the shortest time of anyone I've ever coached. What else are you feeling?"

"You know, Kevin, I'm really grateful for everything you've taught me. I know that I could not have gone as far as I have without your guidance. And that includes what I've learned from you about life–not just skiing."

"Well, buddy, we've come to yet another Champion

Rule: **Be Grateful.** You just showed me that rule on your own. This means you've evolved into a true Champion by learning these rules and applying them in your life. You see, by being grateful, this energy fills you up. You can't hold an opposite or negative emotion when you're filled with gratitude."

"What do you mean?"

"Think about it, can you be mad and grateful at the same time? Can you be jealous and grateful at the same time? Gratitude is the antidote when you find yourself in a negative situation. When you focus on what you're grateful for, that's when you recognize that your journey has meaning."

"I see," Samuel said. "No matter what the outcome is at this tournament, I know I'm just grateful to be here. I'm grateful our paths crossed."

"Me too, buddy. It's been a pleasure watching you grow into the young man you've become. I have an idea for you," Kevin said. "In your next trick run, if you're feeling confident and there's enough time, I want you to try to throw in a 720 turn."

Samuel looked at Kevin in surprise.

"Follow your gut instinct." Kevin smiled.

"Where's Jordan?"

Samuel arrived at the dock for the slalom competition but Jordan was nowhere to be found.

"Jordan is at the urgent care center," Nikki explained. "It looks like he's out of the tournament–he was going down the stairs fast– missed a step and went head first into the stone wall. He's got a possible concussion and a mess of stitches. They're transferring him to the hospital to make sure there's no bleeding in his brain."

Samuel's heart sank. He knew how hard and long Jordan trained for this competition and now he was out.

"Hey Samuel, you're up!'

There was no time to think–Samuel zipped up his wetsuit and hit the water. As he rose to his feet, he felt a surge of energy that he had never felt before.

I'm gonna ride this one for Jordan.

Taking a deep breath, he began his first run, then his second. Samuel was spinning and turning faster than he ever had before, yet time seemed to slow down. In a split second, he remembered Kevin's advice and threw in a 720 turn. Both runs were a personal best and he felt amazing as he tossed the handle at the end.

Samuel wasn't done–the slalom competition was coming up. Samuel closed his eyes and envisioned himself crossing the wake confidently. In his mind, he could see every move.

Fifteen seconds flew by in a flash. He pushed one foot in front of another and glided over the wake. It was one of Samuel's best runs–smooth and effortless. His second run was even faster and better.

"Holy cow, teams, Samuel is on fire!" the announcer boomed. "This young whippersnapper has possibly set a new record over Kevin's unbreakable one! We will go to video review, but we will have results shortly!"

The roar from the crowd was thunderous. Samuel swam to shore and hopped up on the dock. Kevin greeted him with a smile. "Seventeen long years, I held that record, and today you ripped through it! I'm really proud of you. That was some fine skiing out there!"

"I don't know what it was, but it just seemed like everything lined up and the water was like butter," Samuel explained.

"Yup, that's the state of flow," Kevin said. "That's when your training, your passion, and your mission all come together!"

A few minutes later, the announcement was official– Samuel was the new holder of a World record in the slalom event.

In the distance, Zaine stormed off with his head down. He was now out of the running for the Championship.

The race was now down to Kevin...

And Samuel.

CHAPTER 10

Down to the Line

The first rays of the sun broke through the clouds the next morning. Samuel laid in bed reflecting on the journey that brought him around the world in such a short time. He had no expectations at the start of the tournament, yet now he was facing a race to the top against the man who taught him everything.

The championship required a jump distance that Samuel had never reached before. All he had to do was land one decent jump and he would walk away with second place.

Second place was much more than he ever dreamed of for this tournament.

Samuel looked over at Jordan sleeping in the twin bed. Dried blood peeked out through the stitches on his head. He thought back to all the training they did together, the hours and hours in the boat and on the water. It was the friendly, yet fierce, competition between the two of them which drove them to strive for higher and higher ranks.

Samuel grabbed his suit and headed out to the dock. Today was the final day of competition and a new World Champion would emerge.

"Hey son!" Samuel's parents greeted him on the way down to the dock.

"We just wanted to take a minute here and tell you how proud we are of you," his dad said. "You've worked so incredibly hard and advanced so quickly with your skills on the water–"

"And off the water, too," his mom said.

"Ah yes, you've grown into a well-rounded young man! We have just enjoyed watching your progress and seeing the joy on your face after each round."

Samuel hugged his parents. "Thank you for everything you've done–and for making all of this possible for me. I love you both so much."

Samuel walked down to the dock. Kevin, Zaine, and the other finalists were putting their suits on. There wasn't much talk–the mood was somber.

"How's Jordan doing?" Kevin asked.

"He was still sleeping when I left. I didn't know whether or not to wake him up, but I figured it was better if he could wake up on his own."

"Yeah, pal, I can't believe you abandoned me!"

Samuel turned and saw Jordan grinning. "I'm here to cheer you guys on. Wouldn't want to miss seeing who the new champion is gonna be!"

"How's your head?" Samuel asked.

"It's throbbing, but not too bad. I tried to convince Kevin to let me ski."

"Not gonna happen, bro," Kevin said. "Your head took quite a wallop yesterday and we can't knock those brain cells around any further!"

One by one, the skiers hit the jump. One skier took a spectacular crash which knocked his helmet off. After the safety officer cleared the water, it was time for Kevin and Samuel to have their turn.

"Kevin, you're up!" The boat crew idled up to the dock. Kevin slapped on his helmet. "This is it, buddy. I'll see you at the end of this!"

Kevin landed his first and second jumps at a respectable distance. On his final jump, he rose up high and held on to the handle for what seemed like an eternity. Kevin came down late and tumbled head over heels.

The crowd gasped.

"Well, folks, we certainly have a twist on this road to the championship," the announcer said. "Our next skier is Samuel Watkins. This young man started barefooting a few years ago and in a very short time, he has risen up the ranks. Of course, he's been training with the current World Champion, so he has been learning from the best skier in the world. Here's where the pressure comes in– if Samuel lands all three of his jumps with at least one a greater distance than Kevin's– he will be the next World Champion!"

Samuel was already in the water, waiting to go. He closed his eyes. In his mind, he saw his Dream Board with all of the pictures he had posted.

All right butterflies, get yourself in formation–I need you all to move forward in the right direction. We are doing this one for Jordan!

All of a sudden, Samuel felt a wave of peaceful energy wash over him. The outcome didn't matter–he was going to get up and ski with joyful abandon. He loved this sport. The sweet feeling of the water under his feet, the camaraderie of the community, the push to excel– every experience had shaped him into a fine young man. Whether or not he landed a single jump, it was all part of the journey. It was time to put all of his energy into the next three jumps and release the outcome.

Samuel landed his first two jumps cleanly.

"Just one more to get the job done!" the boat driver smiled.

Samuel shot him a big grin. "Let's do it!"

As the ramp became closer, Samuel felt a lightness he had never experienced before. He rose into the air higher and longer than he had ever done before. Pulling his feet under him, he landed on the water and skied away.

The roar of the crowd drowned out the announcer's voice. Samuel couldn't see his distance on the scoreboard. As he swam toward the shore, his teammates were running up to him.

Then Samuel heard the announcer's voice.

"Ladies and gentlemen, we have a new World Champion, Samuel Watkins!"

Jordan grabbed Samuel's hand as he climbed up the dock and wrapped him in a bear hug. "I sure wish it was me–but since it's not, I can't imagine anyone better being the new champion!"

"Thanks, my friend, this championship was definitely a team effort–you were on my mind every minute of it!"

Kevin ran up and grabbed Samuel in a hug. "Congratulations, champ!"

After the awards ceremony, Kevin motioned for Samuel to follow him to a table in the back. "I am really thrilled for you, Samuel, not only for achieving your biggest dream, but also because you followed every single Champion Rule which brought you here today. Now, there's one more rule I want to share with you. It's a rule that not everyone understands–because as human beings, our ego gets in the way and often derails us. The final rule is this: **Be a humble champion.**"

"Does this mean I don't get to brag?" Samuel smiled.

"It goes a bit deeper than that," Kevin chuckled. "You should certainly be proud of being a champion–it's the compilation of your hard work and your dream. As a champion, you have a responsibility to pass your good energy on to others–and to share your wisdom and knowledge."

"Just like you did with me."

Kevin nodded. "You're now part of history–you'll always be known as a champion no matter how many years roll by. There are many eyes on you now. Use the Champion Rules to guide you through your journey ahead–they will never steer you wrong. Create a ripple with your kindness and your knowledge. Share these rules with others–for these rules are the rules of life."

EPILOGUE

Samuel arrived at the ski school and unlocked the doors. A few minutes later, Jordan arrived. The two of them purchased the ski school from Kevin after he retired from the sport. Jordan became a World Champion and the two of them continued to compete fiercely for the champion title between them. The two of them managed a team of ten coaches and all of the boats were full of skiers every day. Skiers flew in from all over the world and often trained for months at a time.

Above the desk was a three-foot high gold frame–a gift from Kevin after Samuel and Jordan purchased the ski school. Inside the frame was a list of The Champion Rules:

Be on Time

Be Coachable

Be Passionate

Be Helpful

Be Committed

Be Persistent

Be Resilient

Be Approachable

Be Grateful

Be a Humble Champion

The Champion Rules were passed on to every student at the school in much the same way that Kevin taught Samuel and Jordan.

"Who do I have in the boat today?" Samuel asked. Jordan looked over the schedule.

"You have Trevor and George–they're visiting from California this week. There's a guy from Tennessee named Steven. We also have a young girl who was watching you on the water earlier in the week. Her name is Melinda–she was pretty fascinated with your tricks on the water and says she wants to learn to do that."

"Who knows, maybe she'll be the next World Champion." Samuel smiled.

ABOUT THE AUTHOR

Karen Putz is known as "The Passion Mentor." She specializes in helping people create more fun, joy, and adventure in the second half of life and beyond. She is the author of multiple books, including the bestseller, "Unwrapping Your Passion, Creating the Life You Truly Want." Karen is also a Chicken Soup for the Soul author, featured in "Find Your Happiness."

Karen is a Certified Passion Test Facilitator personally trained by Janet Attwood, author of The Passion Test.

Karen has been featured in MORE magazine, O magazine, Oprah Daily, and on the TODAY Show.

www.agelesspassions.com

www.yourpassionschool.com

Made in the USA
Middletown, DE
23 December 2022